Copyright © 1995 by Nancy Hall, Inc.
All rights reserved. Published by Scholastic Inc.
Printed in the U.S.A.

ISBN 0-439-45164-7

SCHOLASTIC, MY FIRST HELLO READER!, CARTWHEEL BOOKS, and associated logos and designs are trademarks and/or registered trademarks of Scholastic Inc.

1 2 3 4 5 6 7 8 9 10   24   11 10 09 08 07 06 05 04 03 02

I KNOW KARATE

by Mary Packard
Illustrated by Dee de Rosa

SCHOLASTIC INC.

New York   Toronto   London   Auckland   Sydney
Mexico City   New Delhi   Hong Kong   Buenos Aires

I know karate.
See me bow?

I can block.

This is how.

See my stance?

See my *gi*?

I can jump.

Look at me!

See my form?

I can kick.

I can chop.

See how quick!

Karate is fun.

I can make a monster run!

Here is a monster—
big and scary.

Here is a monster.

My dog, Hairy!

Karate Kids

Point to the kids who are doing karate moves.
Now point to the kid who is doing something different.

Good Sports

Some kids like to do karate. What kinds of activities do you enjoy?

Shadow Play

Look at the shadows. Which pet made each shadow?

Little Riddles

What action word that you do on one foot rhymes with **chop**?

What word that you say on Halloween rhymes with **kick**? *(Here's a hint: It's not a treat.)*

What word that tells the time rhymes with **block**?

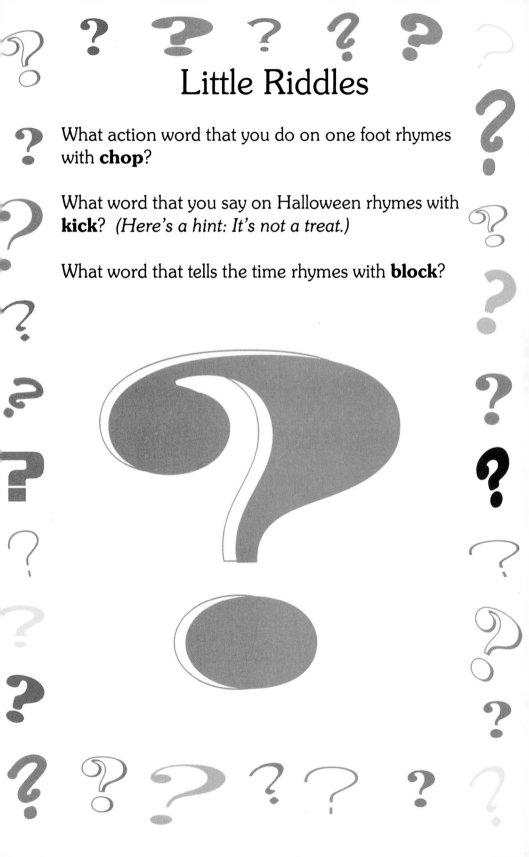

Terrific Me!

Finish these sentences:

I am as fast as _____.

I am as strong as _____.

I am really good at _____.

Karate Action

Here are some action words from this book:

bow   kick

block   chop

jump   run

Can you find these words in the story?

Ask someone to read the story to you. Each time you hear one of these action words, you can do the action!

Answers

(Karate Kids)

This kid is in a ballet position.

(Good Sports)

Answers will vary.

(Shadow Play)

| cat | turtle | bird | rabbit | dog |

(Little Riddles)

The rhyming answers are *hop*, *trick*, and *clock*.

(Terrific Me)

Answers will vary.